Fraud Guide

A simple, no frills, scalable, thought
process for fraud.

1st Edition

by Jonathon Oduwole

This is a guide intended to provide a thought process of how to conduct fraud or financial crime investigations. This guide is not intended to provide legal or other professional advice regarding policies, procedures, statutes, practices, etcetera.

Laws, rules, and practices are constantly changing, therefore, each individual or entity utilizing this guide must perform their own legal research. Each individual or entity utilizing this guide must also perform their own research regarding the rules and policies that they follow, create, and interact with.

Jonathon Oduwole © 2023
ISBN 978-0-9814970-2-0
All Rights Reserved

Preface

This guide was inspired by multiple courses and experiences that I have had while learning fraud investigative techniques.

Throughout this guide, a common theme will be equal weights and measures. When investigating, one must guard against bias, undue influence, favoritism, racism, and all forms of partiality. Unfortunately, this may cause friction within your organization; you must be allied to the truth, not convenience.

This guide is dedicated to all the individuals and organizations that have suffered when utilizing different investigative strategies, then stepping into the unknown to understand the truth.

Table of Contents

Section 1.0

Introduction

A guide can be used to assist individuals in how they are conducting themselves when undertaking an auditing assignment or investigation. Questions that should be asked by a fraud investigator prior to accepting advice or instruction as truth are:

Who is giving the advice?
What are their motives for the advice?
Is the advice applicable?

The guide should be able to assist in proving the credibility of instruction or instructor based on the outcomes of the instruction given.

Section 1.1

Guide Purpose

This instructive guide focuses on case deconstructive techniques relating to fraud investigation. Large scale fraud investigations, which involve multiple entities, whether actors, victims, or other involved subjects require a unique skill set that is often difficult to acquire. Fraud investigation can be civil or criminal in nature. This guide is meant to assist civilian personnel and police agencies alike, no matter the jurisdiction. This guide seeks to relate project management to fraud investigation so that an entity may find culprits, identify security vulnerabilities, and mitigate loss. This guide seeks not to be the only way a fraud investigation can be conducted but does seek to serve as a guide or starting point of how to triage cases, gather information, construct a team centered around the investigation, and if applicable, package information that may assist other entities in furthering a mutual goal in the mitigation of losses.

This guide seeks to have practical examples, these examples are rooted in factual cases. The examples are meant to be illustrations of concepts; they do not serve to be the only situations in which fraud is occurring or how the concepts discussed in this guide can be applied. It is important for fraud investigators to be able to dissect information, including the examples presented in this guide and apply it to the situations that they are tasked with investigating.

Any investigation, including fraud investigation, is meant to uncover nefarious activities, including the acts involved, the entities involved, and is meant to recover losses. All investigations do not lead to uncovering wrongdoing, but may lead to policy failures, legal failures, or other loopholes. Furthermore, these investigations may lead to exonerating individuals that internal or external investigators believe are actors when in fact have no wrongdoing that can be attributed to them.

In a broad sense, auditors, detectives, and certain administrators have the same role, whether they have the authority to legally take individuals liberties away or whether they are fact finders. All these individuals are investigators and seek the truth, whether the truth is convenient or inconvenient for any parties involved. Individuals must be allied to the truth is more important than being allied to power, position, pleasure, or purse.

Section 1.2

Malleability, Policies, and Procedures

The mindset of an investigator is the most crucial factor in investigating. An investigator must be committed to conducting the investigation; a successful investigation does not necessarily lead to a culprit, it may lead to discovering that there is a flawed program, flawed policy, or procedure. A successful investigation may exonerate an individual or entity from wrongdoing or may show antiquated or poor training and a reluctance to follow industry wide standard practice.

Conversely, an investigator may find an individual or entity that is responsible for committing fraudulent activity. In this case, an investigator must be committed because there may be encouragement to rush an investigation or close an investigation. An investigator will face challenges in completing an investigation, both large and small, yet the mindset and malleability of the investigator in this environment is what will allow an investigator to succeed.

Policies and procedures have been mentioned and will continue to be mentioned directly or directly in this guide. This guide is not written with the policies or procedures of entities in mind due to the vast array of rules given by different entities. Entities also have different laws governing them, including Federal, State, Local, Organizational (if members of an association). It is important that investigators understand the entities' rules they are conducting the investigation for.

Investigators have a responsibility in identifying flaws in organizational structure, polices, or practices; most fraud occurs in flaws in verification systems, sometimes complex but usually simple flaws.

Section 1.3

Definitions

While investigations possess a specialized set of circumstances that may have serious legal consequences (civil, administrative, or criminal) the process of investigation can be standardized. The standardization does not come from a myriad of checklists, but from guiding principles that are malleable and adaptive. The following is a list of definitions, while not exhaustive, it will provide a unifying thread throughout this guide.

Administrative Authority- Administrative authority is the ability for an entity to demand or produce records without the need for court orders, such as subpoenas, search warrants, or other legal paperwork. Administrative authority may include the ability to search and seize property for the purpose of furthering an investigation.

Entity – An entity can be a person or organization that is a witness, actor, or victim. An entity can be a business, governmental agency, person, or other organization that may be integral in an investigation.

Scope – Scope is the breadth of the activity that is being investigated. Scope not only includes the activity being investigated, but also the entities, individuals, and techniques that will be needed to complete an investigation.

Investigation – The act of performing an inquiry or a
series of inquiries to determine whether
criminal, civil, or administrative violations
occurred by a specific entity or entities.

Investigator – An investigator is the individual that has
been assigned by an organization to perform an
investigation.

Result – The result is a combination of what
information has been gathered after the
completion of a section or investigation and
what action has been taken (arrest, civil,
administrative, or other action).

End Goal – The end goal is the desired result of a
complete investigation. The end goal may
change as more information develops.

Section – Section describes a portion of an
investigation. The portion of an investigation
will have a goal that will need to be completed
that may determine the end goal.

Action – An action is the usage of techniques that
produces a result.

Triage – Triage is the act of performing preliminary
inquiries prior to the onset of performing an
investigation. The goal of triage is to determine
whether an investigation is merited in a
particular case by a particular entity.

Case – A case is an all-encompassing term of the subject matter of a particular investigation. While an investigation is the process of performing a series of inquiries, the case involves everything within that investigation, from inception to completion. A case can have a singular investigation or multiple investigations.

Merit – Merit is a process that immediately beings once an investigator is made aware of a case. Merit involves an investigator performing a triage on a complaint to determine whether it is worth the expenditure of resources. Determining merit within a case is an ongoing process that may assist in determining what a result should be.

Mitigation- Factors that may limit or reduce culpability, punishment, or other factors involved in an action.

Enhancement – Factors that may increase culpability, punishment, or other factors involved in an action.

Construction – Construction is an investigative technique that utilizes direct knowledge that is gained by becoming a direct witness to the act. Investigations that utilize constructive techniques do not necessarily rely solely on constructive techniques, but the constructive techniques are utilized heavily to determine the current actors.

Deconstruction –Deconstruction is an investigative technique that relies heavily on information that is present to deduce the actors involved. The act has already been committed, and an investigator must examine the information to contextualize what events occurred.

Hybrid- Hybrid is an investigative technique that utilizes both constructive and deconstructive techniques; there is not a specific order that the techniques are utilized but the techniques are utilized in combination in one another.

Fraud-Fraud is the use of deceitful methods to achieve a particular goal. Fraud may be unethical but does not necessarily violate laws, administrative rules, or policy.

Medium –Medium is the method that is utilized to commit fraud.

Jurisdiction – Jurisdiction is whether an entity has the role, right, and responsibility to investigate a particular act or complaint.

Complaint – The complaint is the initial report, external or internal, that alleges the occurrence of fraudulent activities.

Section 2.0

Authority to Conduct Investigations

Individuals, businesses, and the government itself are subject to authority. Those in authority are responsible for creating, administering, and enforcing rules, laws, or regulations. Those that are in authority must understand what their specific role is within an organization and must understand the rules and regulations that give that authority. Those in authority must not step outside of the confines of those rules or there can be grave consequences.

Section 2.1

Internal, Regulatory, Statutory

The authority to conduct investigations can be categorized as internal, regulatory, or statutory. These categorizations can be interconnected; an organization within an organization, or they can describe entities that possess authority to conduct investigations in some areas yet not possess the ability to conduct certain internal investigations.

Statutory Authority is the ability of entities to conduct investigations due to their ability being encoded by State or Federal Law. These investigators can have a great amount of authority yet are limited by laws, rules, or regulations that confine what they are allowed to investigate and further restrain how the investigation can be conducted. Examples are that an investigator that interviews an individual that is suspected of a crime may have the requirement to advise the individual of their constitutional rights prior to an interview or may not be able to interview an individual without an attorney or court recognized guardian present.

Regulatory authority is an authority that is granted by the Federal Government, State Government, Local Government, Organizations/Associations. The member institutions of the governing body may have a pact or are legally subjugated to the rules that the governing body possess as a condition of membership or being able to conduct transactions in business being regulated. The governing body will have the regulatory authority to have investigators that can examine practices, procedures, and related matters to ensure that rules and regulations are being followed. This examination can occur without subpoenas and search warrants.

Internal authority is authority that is granted by the entity that is employing the investigator. An internal investigator will have a vast amount of access to internal information. An organization may allow information to be analyzed by its internal investigators or contractors that have been granted the opportunity to review the information based upon their authority. This information is readily available based upon their internal policies. Internal authority will never exceed superseding Federal or State laws that govern what information may be analyzed and who may view the information.

Section 2.2

Civil Laws, Criminal Laws, Organizations

The differences in these types of laws and rules may best be understood by the penalties that can be levied, the entity that can investigate the allegations, and the jurisdiction/governing body that can hear the case. The next section will briefly discuss these differences between civil, criminal, and organizations' rules or laws.

Civil Laws

Civil laws are laws and rules that are encoded by local, state, or Federal Government. Civil Laws govern how individuals, entities, and government function. Violations of civil laws can be penalized by fines, suspensions, probation (more intense monitoring requirements by regulators), or other types of penalties. Allegations of violations of civil law may arise out of inspection by governmental regulators or entities that are empowered to conduct inspections on behalf of governmental entities. Violations can also be alleged by entities that are conducting business with one another and may have a disagreement concerning contractual obligations or practices. Entities may decide to take this disagreement to a third party recognized by a court or the court itself.

Criminal Laws

Criminal Laws are laws that are encoded by local, state, or federal government. These statutes also govern how individuals, entities, and government function, yet violations of these laws may result in imprisonment and punishment by an individual. Only the government can conduct criminal investigations, prosecute, and imprison individuals. Government not only can imprison citizens of their respective country but can also imprison non-citizens. Imprisonment, fines, probation, parole, deportation, and several different combinations are how the government can decide to punish violation of criminal law. In criminal law, there is an opportunity for accused individuals to defend themselves in a court, local, state, or federal, depending upon the jurisdiction that charges are filed.

Organizational Laws

Organizational Laws are policies that function as always within an organization or entity. Organizational laws are laws that entities must follow to belong to an organization. These laws are not encoded by federal, state, or local laws, but are created by the organization itself. Members of the organization, or the organization itself may vote on laws and enact laws, but violations of these laws are only enforceable by the organization, not by federal, state, or local investigators. Violations of organization rules may result in expulsion from the organization, suspension, fines, or probation. Due to the voluntary nature of being part of an organization, an entity only submits to the organization voluntarily. Not submitting to the fines or penalties may lead to expulsion from the organization. Sometimes entities go to court due to breaking organizational rules, yet it is because there is a greater area of civil or criminal law that was broken, such as contractual obligation disputes.

Section 2.3

Investigator Types

It is important to understand diverse types of investigators, whether they are internal, external, governmental, private entity, empowered to arrest or if they do not possess arrest authority. Investigators that are empowered to arrest individuals are criminal investigators; criminal investigators usually possess limited administrative authority but can arrest individuals for law violations.

There are several types of investigators: internal, civil, and criminal investigators. Internal investigators are investigators that are employed by an organization to determine whether certain policies or procedures have been violated. Furthermore, internal investigators are usually.

Auditors, Inspectors, and other individuals involved in reviewing information are investigators, but their roles are different from Criminal Investigators. These individuals are usually employed directly by the organization, although they can be contracted or statutorily obligated by law. An example of an investigator employed by an organization are internal auditors that ensure funds are being disbursed properly, proper accounting is taking place, or ethical behavior is being followed.

Inspector Generals, a title that is usually utilized in Government (Federal, State, or Local), tend to be involved when major ethical violations occur. Inspector

Generals have much administrative authority, like auditors, which is granted by the organization by which they are employed. Inspector Generals will often investigate the administrative or civil portion of a case, whereas criminal investigators, whether internal (if a governmental agency) or external will investigate whether offenses punishable by a form of imprisonment are applicable options.

Auditors and Inspectors usually are directly employed by organizations that are large, and mandatory reporting obligations to be accountable for financial reports or other things that are of interest to Federal, State, local, as well as their often-independent governing bodies.

Criminal Investigators traverse several jurisdictions: Federal, State, and local. Although Federal investigators may have the largest jurisdiction, they may have limited authority regarding which crimes they are permitted to investigate and may have limited administrative authority. Federal investigators jurisdictions will include all States, Territories, districts, and often, any area where the United States may have a presence, such as U.S. Embassies, Military bases, and other areas that the United States demes under their jurisdiction.

General Investigation Jurisdiction Differences

Investigators at the State level may have a physically large jurisdiction. In this context, size is determined by the physical size of their state. Several states in the United States are larger than several countries. States, such as Alaska, California, Texas, and Montana are larger than most countries. Although state size may influence physical jurisdiction, the influence of the investigative powers of the state may differ due to certain entities being headquartered or transacting business within the state. States, such as California and Texas may have a large jurisdiction but may have an outsized influence due to both states being economic, population, and trading centers of the world. Investigators at the State level will have more authority within their state than Federal entities, but that authority ends at their borders.

Local police agencies, including county-wide agencies, will have a great amount of authority within their jurisdiction due to having the ability to enforce county or local ordinances. These ordinances may carry a harsh financial penalty but do not necessarily include imprisonment as a crime. Local authorities may have a greater amount of administrative or legal tools at their disposal but may also be limited by the resources that they can utilize to investigate or tackle issues. These resources include the ability to recruit, train, and having the luxury of investigators, as well as limitation regarding the funding to have specialized investigative units.

It is important to understand the role of criminal investigators as well as investigators for agencies in general when deciding to determine what types of individuals to include within a fraud investigation. It is important to understand the differences between the Federal, State, and Local jurisdictions so that fraud investigators know who to recruit to assist in an investigation. It is important for criminal investigators to understand whom they may need to recruit or who they need to utilize as references if there is another entity that may be able to fulfill a request better from a fellow criminal investigator or investigator from a private entity.

Section 3.0

Investigative Techniques

Truth is extremely important to the investigator. Always evaluate and corroborate information obtained in an investigation. Ensure the information is valid. When gathering information, ensure that it does not contain bias, and that the information is as thorough as possible.

Section 3.1

Case Constructive Techniques

Case constructive techniques rely on auditors, investigators, police officers (undercover or uniform) cooperating individuals, or witnesses that can attest to an evet occurring in their presence. Case constructive techniques also involve tangible assets that can be physically manipulated, seen, heard, or examined utilizing a variety of techniques. Often, these physical assets are illegal by their very nature; illegal drugs, illegal weapons, illegal identifications, or items that are altered that render them illegal.

There is a prevalence of case constructive techniques that usually involve an investigator or auditor tracking an illegal asset to determine which individual or organizations utilize the illegal asset. Tracking the illegal asset from a constructive perspective can lead to several other entities that are victimized, involved, or are actors themselves. This tracking of the illegal assets or interactions amongst entities can lead to a greater investigation and may lead to other entities that can assist in the investigation being conducted.

Surveillance

Constructive case techniques include conducting surveillance, active monitoring of communications, and firsthand witness accounts. Conducting surveillance on an entity that is known commit violations is a technique that can be labor intensive yet may lead to conclusions that are easier to deduce from everyone, including the investigator, rather than the reliance on experts that can dissect the information.

Cooperating individuals

The usage of cooperating individuals who are a part of the alleged activity can be extremely useful. The cooperating individuals will allow an entity or investigator to actively monitor transactions as well as plan for future transactions so that information can be gathered to further an investigation. Cooperating individuals will need to be managed and approved by organizational policies or governmental regulations, if applicable.

Undercover

An investigator or other individual(s) that is acting under the direction of an investigator that is not actively involved in the alleged nefarious activity can also be a reliable source to gather information. While working undercover can gather the same information as a cooperating individual, the process to integrate an individual operating in an undercover capacity will take a greater amount of time. Taking a greater amount of time to integrate an individual acting in an undercover capacity can cost a victim organization several thousands of dollars and may not be worth the effort.

Personal Observation

An investigator, not in an undercover capacity or without the use of Cooperating individuals may observe the violations in-person, without any type of cunning involved. The actor in the unethical or immoral activity involved knows that the individual observing the activity is an investigator yet is confident in their ability in not having any negative consequences to their actions.

Section 3.2

Case Deconstructive Techniques

Case deconstructive techniques are techniques that are utilized when there is an ample amount of information, but the investigator must contextualize the information. There may not be several witnesses, yet a skillful investigator can carefully examine the information and deduct what events occurred. Examples of diverse types of investigators that utilize deconstructive case techniques are homicide investigators, crash investigators, and fraud investigators. This list is not a complete list but is illustrative of the type of investigators that routinely utilize case deconstructive techniques. The purpose of this guide is to focus on fraud investigators, yet the concepts may be applicable for investigators that examine several diverse types of information to deduce what events have occurred and if those events constitute violations of administrative rules, laws, or policy.

Section 3.3

Record Analysis

Record analysis requires dissecting physical documents or electronic data. Physical and electronic data can involve diverse types of information, including coordinates, dates, times, names, financial transactions, financial institutions, contact information, addresses and other information valuable to an investigation.

Physical Document Analysis

Physical Document analysis involves analyzing documents that may possess valuable information for patterns. Analyzing documentation that is kept by the victim entities, third parties, or other sources is a valuable tool that investigators may utilize to positively identify culprits as well as flaws or gaps in security. There are several ways that documents can be obtained, including simple requests to court authorized searches and seizures.

Drawbacks of physical document analysis are storing the physical volume of information if it is copied, or the source material is taken. Physical storage space can be difficult and analyzing such documents can be cumbersome. Physical document analysis can also face the challenge of physical preservation, care, and delicate handling.

Electronic Data Analysis

Electronic data analysis involves analyzing information stored electronically. Electronic data and physical documents possess the same information; electronic data is usually collected and stored for various purposes, including marketing purposes for the company. Electronic data can also be cumbersome and possess its own storage challenges. While the data may not utilize physical space, electronic storage can be a challenge. Furthermore, analyzing electronic data requires special tools for extraction and analysis. While the goal is still the same as physical data analysis, the way the analysis is performed is different.

Interviews

Utilizing interviews during a strict deconstructive matter is different than utilizing interviews in a case constructive manner. The use of interviews can be extremely important when conducting case deconstruction. Interviews can assist in providing context to schemes, actions, and motivation. Often, Interviews, when utilized for case deconstruction are not necessarily integral in conducting an initial investigation but may be integral when an investigator decides to expand the scope of an investigation beyond the initial parameters.

Time Estimates

Unlike other styles of project management, it is difficult to formulate time estimates when conducting investigations. The best project management estimates are based upon previous investigations. Time estimates given from the overall investigation will comprise the aggregation of certain distinct elements, including the volume of information being requested from other entities, the victim organization, and the subject matter of the information should be utilized to complete time estimates.

Volume of Information

The volume of information being requested from entities is important in determining the time estimate for a particular section of an investigation or the overall investigation. The volume of information involves the number of documents, items, or other pertinent information that is needed or requested by an investigator to analyze. The entities that are receiving the request may have to utilize different systems to retrieve, categorize, and have internal staff review the information to ensure compliance with the request or demand. This process is affected by the size, technological state, and internal/external processes of the entity. The size of the entity may lead to either rapid or slower responses to requested material.

The entity may have several assets (companies or divisions) that the information is drawn from requiring time to gather. This information will still need to be processed, vetted, and sent via a secure route to ensure compliance with the request. The secure route may include certain types of electronic mail, physically secured service, or hybrid approach that involves both physical and electronic information being sent to the requestor.

The technological state of the entity refers to whether the entity involved will have the technology to send the requested document via secured electronic mail. Often, entities still possess items in only a physical format that requires the items to be sent physically to a secure location. While it only takes moments to send items electronically, if the items are categorized properly, it may take several weeks or months to find the items, replicate the items, then send them to the investigator.

The internal and external processes involved can be minute or grand. The internal process once a request is received may involve the reception of a request, it being routed to the proper authority within an organization, analyzed, approved, then the request for various pieces of information being gathered. This request may also employ an external authority subcontracted by an entity to review the information to ensure compliance with the information yet not providing more than what is requested to protect the company as well as any other clients involved in the request.

Information Collected from Victim Organization

The victim organization is the entity that has been defrauded out of the benefits that are legally owed to it. The victim organization can be large or small, whether it has thousands of employees or one, often, it is the entity that is alleging an unlawful activity, civil or criminal, has happened. The victim organization may affect time estimates due to how robust their information gathering requirements are, which is governed by both external policies (federal or state laws/administrative policies) and internal administrative policies. The more information that is gathered, the more information can be initially analyzed to determine the actors that are responsible.

If the victim organization is the reporting entity, depending upon the size of the entity, it will have a vast amount of information that leads it to believe that unethical or unlawful activity is occurring. The entity will collect vast amounts of information to determine how it can better serve its customers, provide accurate billing, and a good customer experience. This is the same data that can be exploited for analysis to find patterns of behavior for suspected actors involved.

Subject Matter

The subject matter of an investigation is descriptive of what the investigation is primarily seeking to discover. While investigations may possess several infractions of internal policy, criminal law, or civil law, the subject matter is describing what the investigator is seeking to uncover. An example is that an individual may be rewarding contracts to entities without proceeding through a process that is required by law or administrative rules that is present within State, Federal, or local government. If an individual(s) within an entity rewards these contracts there may be an investigation that occurs after the discrepancy is found or a complaint lodged by a multitude of entities.

Within this context, several violations may have occurred. Usually, if there is a criminal component, such as the act of purposely rewarding contracts without proper oversight or going through the process prescribed by an entity that has proper authority, there will be a criminal complaint lodged. While the criminal complaint may be lodged, it may be lodged by an entity that does not have proper jurisdiction or that may not have the resources to investigate the matter.

Section 4.0

Data Types

Several types of data will be gathered during an investigation. Data can be categorized in multiple ways; in this section, data types will be categorized as transactional location, and identification.

Section 4.1

Transactional Data

There are diverse types of data an investigator will need to utilize for various purposes. Some of the reasons an investigator will collect these diverse types of data is to corroborate information, validate complaints, generate leads, and complete an investigation. Transactional data shows the relationship between entities.

Transactional data is data that shows that an exchange occurred between two or more parties. This exchange can be for economic benefits, quid pro quo, theft, or other exchanges that are deemed to be beneficial to at least one of the parties involved. Transactional data can show the patterns of illicit actors, flaws within policies, as well as unusual patterns that may lead to the culprit who committed fraud.

Examples of transactional data are statements from financial institutions, auditing statements, receipts, wiring reports, bank securities act information, purchase orders, request for service made by entities, etcetera. Transactional data does not necessarily need to involve a commodity or financial resources, transactional data may show service-related transactions or requests.

Section 4.2

Location Data

Location data is information that shows the area where an activity took place. Location data may contain physical addresses, lot numbers, or other types of information that specifically identifies an area. Location data may also refer to stored electronic data that identifies a general service provider or specific device where the information originated from. These devices include but are not limited to servers, computers, or cellular phones. Location data is extremely useful when attempting to locate witnesses or evidence.

Section 4.3

Identification Data

Identification data is information that identifies entities that are responsible for performing certain actions when they encounter the subject matter of inquiry or investigation. Identification data can be physical or electronic. Physical identification data includes governmental identification documents, such as driver's licenses, passports, identification cards, visas, etcetera. Physical identification may also be self-reported in job applications, benefit applications, or other documents that are voluntarily submitted by individuals.

Electronic identification data can be customer data that is electronically stored by an entity. This information can also overlap with physical identification data. Such as an electronic copy of a driver's license that was submitted as part of an electronic job or loan application. While there is a physical driver's license, there is also an electronic copy as well.

Documents containing Identification data, location data, and transactional data can overlap. These items are not mutually exclusive and often are contained within the same document or groups of documents being analyzed. Understanding these diverse types of data may assist an investigator in being more efficient in determining how to employ different investigative techniques.

Section 5.0

Intake

Performing intake is one of the preliminary steps that organizations must undertake when determining whether an investigation will take place, a case rejected, or a referral to another entity occur. This section will deal with information intake, triage, and case adoption.

Section 5.1

Information Intake

Information intake is the act of receiving information to determine whether the information being received is within the purview of the investigator, whether there was a violation of law or internal practices, and whether the allegations are worth the effort that is going to be expended in investigating the complaint. Information Intake is the beginning stage of triage that is an ongoing process through the investigation. The most important triage is the initial triage.

Section 5.2

Triage

This section of the guide is going to focus on the role of performing preliminary inquiries to determine whether an issue brought to an investigator meets criteria that would allow an investigator to formally adopt the issue into a case. The preliminary triage will involve several factors, including the nature of the complaint, the entities involved, as well as the impact of the potential allegations derived from the complaint.

The initial triage should review the information contained in the complaint. This initial triage performed by an investigator will be more in depth than the intake apparatus. The initial intake triage should only be concerned with whether the entity is the appropriate entity to conduct the investigation. Once making it past the intake triage, the initial triage is performed by the investigator.

Intake triage vs. Investigator triage

Triage should occur at various levels of an organization. Triage begins with legal obligations, authority that are mandated by laws, statutes, or rules that are issued by a governing organization.

Organizations are unique in how they create systems involving the intake of a complaint, disbursement of a complaint to an investigator (which may involve several steps), to the completion of the investigation of a complaint, if an investigation takes place. If organizations are large enough, they will have an internal or external entity that will review complaints regarding fraud or other types of impropriety.

Initial Triage

The role of the individuals performing the initial triage is to determine whether there are violations that fall within the purview of the organization. If the complaint falls within the purview of the organization, another assessment should be made. An assessment should be made to determine if the organization has the expertise to conduct the investigation, even if they have legal authority, statutes, and rules that allow them to investigate the complaint. It is possible that expertise is one of the leading factors in determining to divert an investigation to another entity; not necessarily determining that an investigation should not take place but answering the question of whether the triaging organization is the one to perform it. Individuals performing the initial triage are there to assist investigators in making their burden lighter. Depending upon the organizational structure, the initial triage may lead to further review and approval by supervisors where the complaint leads to further review or is rejected.

Investigator Triage

When an investigator is given a complaint to investigate, they must also perform a triage. An investigator's triage may take longer to perform than the initial triage because an investigator may have other parameters that they must meet to determine whether case adoption will occur. Factors that an investigator is going to consider are the same as the initial triage; statutes, rules, and expertise, yet will also examine whether the investigative efforts expended are worth the result of the investigation. The reason there is an overlap in the investigator triage and initial triage is because an investigator must not assume that the initial triage understands the parameters that the organization is operating in; this serves as a secondary review to protect the organization from breaking organizations rules, statues, or laws that require an organization to investigate alleged fraudulent or improper activities. The investigator triage is a crucial factor in determining whether a complaint leads to case adoption. Depending upon the organizational structure, the investigator's initial triage and determination may lead to further review by supervisors or the investigator's determination may be final.

The nature of the complaint

The nature of the complaint is a summary of facts contained within a complaint that have not been investigated or verified. The nature of the complaint will involve allegations of wrongdoing, the actors responsible, the location(s) of the incident(s), as well as harm that has been caused.

Entities Involved

The entities involved are the entities that are alleged to be victimized, affected, or are the actors. The entities involved will have an interest in the investigation because they may be affected civilly or criminally. An entity may be involved due to storing items, although they are not necessarily a victim of the crime, they may be required to participate in a civil or criminal process to produce records or other items.

Determining the entities involved will assist in ascertaining the legal authority needed to obtain/compel the release of information, the internal policy, or identifying the appropriate authorities that can investigate the allegations.

Location of the Incident

The location of the incident is where the alleged incident occurred. The location of the incident may be multiple locations, including where physical or electronic transactions occurred, where items are stored or transmitted, and where the corporate headquarters where the business is legally registered.

Harm

The harm that has been caused can be a single factor or a variety of factors, including the loss of revenue, customer confidence, insurance premiums, the cost to recover losses, legal fees, monetary loss, and other costs that are not specifically listed.

Conclusion of Triage

The amount of information needed to complete a triage of a case may depend upon several factors. The factors may include the jurisdiction of the organization, the resources that the organization or investigator has at their disposal, the length of time allotted to complete the triage (organizational policies or governmental factors such as statute of limitations), or other factors that are not listed. Concluding the triage may lead to a formal investigation, a referral to a separate entity, or dismissal of the complaint.

Triage Conclusion - Jurisdiction

Triaging cases that organizations participate in may have several factors, such as internal policies, funding, and personnel.

Internal Policies – Internal policies should cover a wide variety of factors when considering a case. These factors will include the threshold of the amount that was stolen or unaccounted for, the role of the organization, and the

Resources – Resources include the authority or ability to compel information internal to the organization conducting the triage and external. The time allotted to complete a triage; the more complex a case, the more information that is needed to complete a triage.

Personnel- The personnel involved in conducting the triage will need the necessary experience or training to understand what information is needed to proceed with an investigation, refer the case to another entity, or to dismiss without referral.

Referral-Sending the case to another entity may be the best option if it is determined that the entity receiving the referral is best equipped to manage the case.

Dismissal-Dismissing a case after triage may lead to a complete dismissal with no further investigation or may lead to a referral to another entity, whether internal or external.

Section 5.3

Case Adoption

Once a case passes triage and meets the requirements for case adoption, there are steps that organizations may take to begin formal investigation. Determining the type of case, civil, criminal, or administrative, then assigning the lead investigator based upon determination. The complexity includes how the acts were committed, which entity and how many were defrauded, as well as the total amount fraud that occurred or was attempted are all considered when determining the complexity. Once this is determined, an investigator should be assigned based upon these factors.

Lead Investigator

A Lead Investigator is the investigator that is primarily responsible for the investigation. The lead investigator should conduct their own triage to determine if they are the individual or entity that is responsible for investigating a case. The lead investigator may utilize a wide variety of techniques, including case constructive, case deconstructive, and hybrid techniques. The lead investigator is the project manager who will be responsible for the success or failure of the project, the project being the investigation.

Essential elements of being a lead investigator are to conduct their own triage, determine the subject matter of the investigation (what is being investigated), and the team being selected to assist in the investigation. If an inquiry becomes an investigation, it is important for an organization and investigator to understand that the results may lead to no violations being found; this is not necessarily a waste of time, effort, or human resources, but may be fruitful in understanding how certain rules, laws, or policies may need to be implemented.

Investigator Triage

Depending upon the size of an investigation, the organization conducted a generic triage to determine whether the allegations are worth the effort to investigate. Certain claims internal to the organization (a claim by an employee or contractor) or externally (a complaint lodged by an external entity) may be worthless, yet the allegation's brevity may lead to the necessity of adoption as a case for an investigator.

No matter what the investigation, if it passes organizational triage, and is assigned as a case to an investigator, the investigator must conduct their own triage. An investigator should have proper experience within their field to determine whether they are the correct entity to conduct the investigation and or make recommendations as to the proper entities that should be involved.

Section 6.0.

Investigatory Information Gathering Tools

There are several diverse types of tools that are available to investigators. Investigatory tools may vary based upon the position of the investigator, the particular entity involved in the investigation, and the availability of the tools. This section will cover types of information gathering, such as the use of nonlegal processes, legal processes, and witness interviews.

Section 6.1

Nonlegal processes

Nonlegal information gathering techniques are processes that do not require legal backing. These techniques rely heavily on open-source information. Certain databases are open for review, such as certain types of tax information available via government databases, websites owned by the entity in question, as well as personal websites or social media that is open in scope. Open websites can assist investigators in determining relationships, location, and the demeanor of the subjects of investigations. Nonlegal processes also involve requests made by investigators. Although a request for information may be formal, it is not a legal process; entities can reject formal or informal requests for information and have no requirement to respond. There are no formal penalties for rejecting these types of requests nor is there any type of recourse for investigators making these requests after rejection. There are certain types of information that an entity may be able to release based upon formal request, often, depending upon the subject matter, there are laws, both state and federal, that require legal processes, therefore, an entity may not be able to comply with the request, even when cooperating with an investigation.

Section 6.2

Legal Processes

Administrative Authority

There are several diverse types of legal processes; the most common that investigators will utilize are subpoenas, search warrants, and administrative searches. These tools are utilized by diverse types of investigators, divided into civil or criminal. Civil investigators will utilize a great amount of administrative authority if they are employed by a regulatory agency, association, or other type of entity that possesses authority within an industry. Administrative authority allows entities to conduct searches without the need for search warrants or subpoenas. Administrative authority will still have limits yet does allow for the entities conducting the search or investigation to gather valuable information. Failure for entities subject to these administrative searches to comply may result in fines, suspension, or expulsion from an organization or industry.

Administrative Subpoenas

There are diverse types of subpoenas. Administrative subpoena(s) issued by agencies, or attorneys may require entities to comply if there is an official investigation or proceeding occurring. Administrative subpoenas usually do not need any type of judicial review, such as the review of a magistrate or an attorney. Later, once criminal or civil action takes place, the authority and usage of the administrative subpoena may be challenged. Furthermore, while administrative subpoenas can be a great tool because they can be issued quickly, they may not give the investigator a vast amount of information, especially when utilizing administrative subpoena for electronic customer data. Entities that are served with administrative subpoenas may notify customers that their records have been requested by entities. This can be circumvented by having an authorized legal entity, such as a magistrate, signing a nondisclosure order, ordering the affected or served entity to not notify the customers. This practice can be useful but may take time to find the proper magistrate or legal entity to provide the nondisclosure order.

Search Warrants & Grand Jury Subpoenas

Specifically, Investigators that are employed by criminal justice agencies have tools that are not available to those that are conducting civil investigations. These tools require an investigator to swear to the known information, their experiences, training, and inferences that come from those combinations to deduce that the results of the court processes will lead to evidence.

Investigators utilize these tools because they compel entities to provide information. This information can be utilized as evidence or utilized as leads to finding where evidence may be discovered. Furthermore, the usage of search warrants allows investigators to determine how entities have conducted their business by allowing investigators to gather more information to examine.

Grand Jury Subpoenas are issued as an investigative tool for prosecutorial officers or investigators at police agencies. Grand Jury subpoenas are a legal tool that have strict nondisclosure orders attached due to the secretive nature of grand Juries. The secretive nature of grand juries is to ensure the integrity of an investigation or inquiry and for the protection of jurors, so that they are not wrongly influenced or threatened.

Section 6.3

Witness Accounts

Witness accounts, especially when garnered from employees, may involve individuals being compelled for their testimony. When witness accounts are administratively invoked, employees may be required to assist in an administrative investigation or risk administrative penalties given by their employer.

These penalties include but are not limited to demotion, relocation, or termination. When administratively compelling witness accounts, employers may have a greater latitude when dealing with private entities. When administratively dealing with public employees, it may be more difficult to compel employee testimony due to the nature of governmental entities having certain constitutional obligations to ensure they do not trample the rights of individuals if the administrative investigation has criminal implications.

There is also a possibility that a criminal investigation is occurring. If a criminal investigation is occurring, this will be performed by local, state, or federal entities. When a criminal investigation is occurring, these agencies may interview witnesses, actors, and other personnel to determine the individuals involved as well as determining what the normal processes are. During a criminal investigation, an individual does not have to provide information although investigators may utilize certain tools to obtain information.

Section 7.0

Team Construction

When performing larger investigations, it will be more efficient and less burdensome to select capable individuals who are competent in their areas. Team determination, scaling, and roles are important for an investigator to consider. Investigators do not need to maintain the same team throughout an investigation and may add or subtract team members throughout an investigation once their tasks are performed.

Section 7.1

Team Determination

When conducting a medium or large-scale investigation, an investigator will need to bring several individuals together that have diverse experiences and knowledge within the subject matter. Due to fraud and financial crime investigations usually having multiple industries involved, an investigator will need to determine which industries and entities possess information that can be utilized to determine how illegal or unethical activity occurred, and the individual(s) responsible. The initial team to be constructed should be developed throughout the triage stage.

Conducting the triage of a case should provide enough information to determine what the subject matter of the investigation will center upon. The subject matter of the investigation should possess a major civil, administrative, or criminal violation for the basis of investigation. Although there may be numerous infractions in one or all areas, it is best practice to focus on one major violation as that violation will usually have the most information to dissect. An example is that if an investigator receives information regarding the fraudulent use of credit card information to obtain goods from a specific store, the credit card company should be contacted.

After analysis of credit card information or retail store data, an investigator may find that a pattern exists. This pattern can be where the activity occurs, what medium is utilized to commit the activity, when certain personnel are working in certain positions, or any other myriads of combinations that pertain to location, personnel and etcetera.

If available, the fraudulent use of credit card information involves the purchase or attempted purchase of goods or services from certain entities. These entities may be contacted to determine the extent of the activity. These entities may possess certain identifying information, such as membership information, email addresses, physical addresses, or may contain surveillance footage that will identify individuals, vehicles, or other identifiable items.

From the above example, there are many entities that may be contacted that an investigator can build a team with. Individuals that are in certain companies, such as retail, credit card, governmental, or other private sources may be placed on your fraud team to deconstruct a case.

Section 7.2

Scaling

Scaling through the triage process and initial investigation, an investigator should develop a basic understanding of how large the investigation is going to be. Throughout the triage process, an investigator should be evaluating and re-evaluating the information that was presented and is continually being collected. There should be constant analysis of information. The purpose of gathering information in an investigation is normally to find more sources of information, so that the information that is unknown can become known. Knowing information leads to finding who is responsible for the losses, whether these losses are merely from an external or internal actor involved, and where those resources that were improperly coopted located.

There should be an initial idea of how large the investigation is going to be; an initial scale is usually going to involve the investigator, or an investigator or analyst. If the investigator deems the investigator needs more individuals with expertise in the subject matter, the investigation should be scaled larger. This scaling ensures that the investigator has enough individuals with expertise to properly analyze information and inform the investigator of what can be concluded or is concluded from analysis of the information. At times, an investigator may enlarge an investigation based upon the information received. Anticipating the need for more resources is good yet should be scrutinized by the investigator. The investigator needs to understand what resources are needed, why those resources are needed, and the duration of those resources.

Once an investigation has taken the steps to build the larger structure needed to gather and analyze information an investigator must continue to incorporate that data into their evaluation. There should come a time when the investigator decides the scope of the investigation, what or who is being investigated, and whether the investigative team should continue forward or whether there needs to be changes made to the investigative team. These changes may include incorporating more individuals, changing the individuals or entities involved in the investigation, or downscaling the size of the investigation due to the subject matter.

Section 7.3

Roles

Roles are what each team member is meant to fulfill. Roles may have some overlap in expertise, yet their responsibilities and purview should be quite different. A lead investigator's role is to determine if there has been a violation of policy, law, or rule with the information presented by the investigative team. The lead investigator is responsible and will bear the weight on the

The role of an analyst is to analyze specific portions of information gathered by the investigative team. An example is that an analyst may examine financial statements, leasing information, or other documents that have been gathered by the investigative team. An analyst may examine the information to find patterns or tendencies by those entities involved.

Section 8.0

Prosecution

Prosecution requires investigators to consider gathering more information. This information is needed because the threshold or burden is greater than internal administrative policies, regulatory policies, or civil policies. The investigator must understand and contextualize the information relating to criminal acts; this must be completed within a certain time. This may be further compounded by the scope of the crime as well as determining the impact of the prosecution.

Section 8.1

Timing

Timing involves when an entity and specific portions of an entity are notified of potential violations. These violations normally have a statute of limitations attached. The statute of limitations is how long an entity can be held responsible from the time in which violations occurred. An example is that certain criminal activity may not have a statute of limitations, such as homicide, whereas certain criminal activity, such as certain types of theft, fraud, or wire fraud may have a statute of limitation from two years to ten years. These statutes of limitations are influenced by a wide number of variables, such as the impact or quantifiable amount taken, the rules in place, or how the unlawful action occurred.

It is important that an investigator receives information in a timely manner, especially if the act occurred several years prior to it being discovered. An investigator and entity responsible for triage will first examine if there has been a violation of rules or statutes. Next, an investigator will also determine if there is enough time to complete an investigation that will positively identify the actor(s) responsible. If there is not enough time to positively determine the actor(s) responsible, an investigator will note what violations or rules were violated, and why there is not enough time to positively identify the actor(s) responsible. This information should be passed to the organization employing the investigator so that the organization can decide if they still want to proceed with the investigation despite whether there are consequences.

The reason an organization may want to complete the investigation, despite there not being a penalty attached or chance to directly recoup losses (financial or otherwise), is to determine how the losses occurred and how they could have been prevented or mitigated. Some questions that a victim organization may want answers are the following:

1. Are there internal processes, (rules or procedures) that exist that could have detected the actions in question?
2. If internal processes exist, are they properly followed?
3. If they were followed, is there a need to modify the rules or procedures?
4. If they were not followed, was this act intentional, unintentional, or negligent?
5. Was there proper supervision and verification procedures in place?
6. Are there external processes, such as external audits, which exist and are those processes being followed?
7. Is there a possibility that an external organization is also following proper reporting procedures?
8. Is there a possibility that some of the actor(s) involved are still employed by the organization?
9. Was there a violation of contractual obligations by the entities involved?

Section 8.2

Scope

The scope of the crime refers to the gravity of the offense, the affected individuals, and commonality of the crime. The gravity of the offense is how grave the violation of statutes, rules, or laws are. The totality of the circumstances, a phrase that is common in criminal justice, is the usage of all factors involved to determine mitigating and enhancing factors. Determining the gravity of the offense is an inexact science, yet certain factors are set, such as the mental state of the actor or victim (if applicable), the impact of the crime on the victim (including large corporations), and the general circumstances surrounding the motivations of the actor.

An example of this is an individual that steals fifty dollars' worth of groceries versus an individual that is in a trusted position and utilizes their trusted position to steal fifty dollars. While stealing fifty dollars' worth of groceries may not be a lot of money, if the motivating factor were to feed a family, this may be a mitigating factor. The individual stealing the groceries may have to pay fifty dollars back or serve a less severe penalty. An individual that utilized their trusted position to steal fifty dollars, such as someone who works in a position where they are responsible for the accounting of funds for a corporation may receive a more severe penalty. The enhancing factor is that they are in a trusted position, knowing that their responsibility is to account for the funds for an entity. If a more severe penalty occurs, it is so that the actor involved and others in general know that when working for an entity and knowing those responsibilities, that they should not steal while the individual stealing groceries may be viewed as abnormal circumstances requiring immediate action, even if those actions are not necessarily complete correct.

Section 8.3

Impact of prosecution

The impact of prosecution is something that is considered by organizations internally as well as by State or Federal investigators and Prosecutors. The impact of prosecution is related to the effect of unlawful activity on a particular area (physically), financially, and how individuals acting in a lawful manner would fare.

Focusing efforts on prosecuting one individual who is committing fraud using a fraudulent identification to obtain a $300.00 loan versus prosecuting an individual who is utilizing multiple identifications to obtain multiple $100,000.00 loans is an example of how investigators or prosecutors may triage cases to determine which case is worth the effort.

Section 9.0

Recovery

Recovering loss can be difficult. An investigator must identify accounts, trace transactions, and then recover funds, often through a legal mechanism but sometimes through voluntary course.

Section 9.1

Identifying accounts

The identification of accounts is of paramount importance. Distinguishing what individual or entity owns the account involves extrapolating information obtained from the results of legal documentation, such as search warrants or subpoenas that were issued to entities that possess the financial information of the subject being investigated. This information may also be voluntarily divulged if it is deemed by a victim organization to defraud the organization or as a means of making the organization holding the account potentially culpable. An example is that an organization that holds an account, such as a bank, may not be actively committing a crime, such as money laundering, but may be fined or responsible if certain information is not being reported. Information required to be reported includes but is not limited to transfers of funds above a certain amount or suspicious, structured transactions. This report will include who owns the account, the bank where the suspicious transaction occurred, and when the transactions were recorded.

Furthermore, accounts that are used by an actor providing false or synthetic identification information that is utilized by an actor to obtain financial benefits while harming an institution, such as obtaining credit or loans, by not paying the loan or credit, may be closed.

Section 9.2

Tracing Transactions

To trace transactions, an investigator needs to identify the entity that possesses the records, the accounts being traced, and specific time frames for the transactions that have occurred. Identifying the entity that possesses the records may happen in a multitude of ways; this includes identification of the records being revealed by the subject of the investigation, the victim entity, or a third-party entity, such as FINCEN, compiling information regarding self-reported suspicious transactions within financial related business.

Third Party Tracing

An example of a third-party reporting information to FINCEN is if ABC Financial Institution examines transactions coming from an account holder, showing that there are multiple transactions in a short amount of time (one week) that are just below the required $10,000.00 reporting level. This information is reported to FINCEN because it may be a sign of money laundering and structuring of transactions to avoid detection. While the financial institution or institutions may report the account information, this information is reported to FINCEN, not necessarily directly to a justice agency or regulatory agency.

An entity responsible for performing investigations, if members of FINCEN, may utilize the information to assist in a current investigation or may probe further to determine whether criminal or regulatory fraud has occurred. An investigator may contact the institution reporting the information but will need to utilize legal documentation to obtain the information on the specific accounts or transactions.

Third Party Reporting is extremely useful and helpful in unlawful activity reported, furthermore, the third-party information can reveal patterns, especially when multiple institutions are reporting the same individuals or entities committing suspicious activity.

Section 9.3
Recovering funds

The recovery of funds may occur in several ways. Funds may be voluntarily relinquished by an actor or business; normally to avoid criminal prosecution and limit civil exposure. A company may utilize non-legal means to compel payment, such as payment requests or payment demand letters to the entities. A suspension of the account may occur, and the utilization of the account or the services provided by the institution may cease until the funds are returned.

There are several examples of court orders that require entities to reimburse institutions or individuals that are victims of fraud. Court orders will be obtained after a party alleging a violation of civil law, including contractual agreements, goes to a court for a resolution, whether that resolution is through a civil trial, voluntary mediation, or court order mediation. It is important to note that depending upon the jurisdiction, some mediation, whether voluntary or mandatory may not be binding but may be a necessary step prior to filing a lawsuit alleging wrongdoing.

Another court order is a search and seizure warrant. A search and seizure warrant usually possesses three distinct parts, a warrant, an affidavit for the warrant, and an item known as a return. The warrant section will command the investigator to search in a particular area for object(s) or items related to a crime, and to seize those items. The next section is the warrant affidavit. The warrant affidavit is a section where the investigator explains the criminal activity that is believed to be occurring, the area or object to be searched, and the explain what items are to be seized and why they would be important within the context of an investigation. The last section is known as a return, the return is the section that is filled out after the execution of a search warrant to explain what items were taken.

The warrant and affidavit are taken before a magistrate as prescribed by law and are then approved as evidenced by a signature from a judge. There are nuisances to search warrants, including jurisdiction considerations, the entity that is being searched and the item(s) that are being seized. Seizures of bank accounts or financial assets held by an entity usually require search and seizure warrants when relating to fraud or financial crimes.

Conclusion

It is important for fraud managers, supervisors, and leaders to walk with integrity because they will have influence on how organizations, individuals, and entities, internal or external to the fraud community treat the findings of investigations. Furthermore, ethics, great investigators, and organizations are more than subjective criteria or erroneous measures of success.

Growth of Fraud

Fraud and financial crimes have existed throughout the existence of man and will continue as long as man exists in our current capacity. Fraud has always been a threat to individuals and societies due to the massive amount of damage that can be done financially as well as physically. Selling deceptive products utilized in construction, deceptive self-defense products, or selling securities and shares of corporations that do not lead to loss of life, finances, and finally, increased stress.

The ways to commit fraud will continue to grow with the increase of technology. Fraud, committed with tangible objects, such as counterfeit money or physical identification will be prominent, yet the increased use of financial transactions will make it easier for an individual committing fraud to have greater distancing behavior.

Fraud Manager/Investigator Responsibilities

Management is responsible for placing investigators in a position to succeed. Managers must select investigators that can succeed by being able to provide training and recognize the ability investigators possess. Management cannot succumb to poor measures of what may make a successful person a great auditor or investigator. These poor measures of success are often displayed with policies (both written and unwritten) that possess erroneous criteria for certain positions, such as having a personal relationship with an individual, or mis contextualizing statistical information that is utilized justify hiring an individual or firm to perform a task.

Organizations must have reasonable expectations and utilize reasonable metrics of success to determine whether an individual should be selected to be an investigator and determine what role an investigator may be utilized in within that organization. While this may be a basic premise, several organizations are failing, both public and privately, to effectively select an investigator that could uncover fraud, then examine failures of an organization that may need to update its practices or procedures to limit future liability.

Managers, investigators, and entities must understand the way fraud and financial crimes are committed against entities will continue to evolve; what will not change is the reason individuals commit these acts is to gain some type of benefit. Continual training, recognition in trends, and understanding verification processes within an organization are general ways that investigators can prevent or limit exposure, and in some cases, recover funds as well as bring those responsible to prosecution.

Practical Example One

Suppose an entity, JJ Financial Institution, disburses a loan to an individual claiming to represent a business. The individual representing the business brings identifying documents of the corporation, as well as identifying documents for himself.

After a while, the loan is never paid, and the entity decides to issue letters to the entity demanding payment. It was found by internal investigators that the entity never existed, and that the documentation was false.

As an internal investigator, how can you positively identify whether the identifying documents are real or false?

Contact entities that can assist in identifying information, such as a law enforcement agency or the entity that issued the documents. If the documents are false, the entity that the document fraudulently represents is a victim.

It is important to develop personal contact with individuals in agencies so that information can flow efficiently.

What are specific identifiers on the document?

When an investigator finds that a document is false, such as a business, an investigator should examine that document closely. There is a great possibility that there are specific identifiers, such as the name of the entity issuing the document, the name of the individual, specific numbers identifying the individual, entity issuing the document, and specific document number. There may also be address information for a business or individual, as well as contact information via email, or phone number.

This information is valuable because it gives an investigator a tangible place where surveillance may occur, or legal processes requiring the divulgence of electronic custom data for email, phone data, etcetera.

As an internal investigator, what documents can you turn over to a third party?

Understand policies, procedures, and laws governing the release of documentation, especially if the documentation is sensitive in nature. The documents may be fraudulent, but legal documentation may be required for the release of the information to a third party. This legal documentation may come from the entity affected or the third party receiving the documentation.

What policies, procedures, and laws must you adhere to?

While certain documents can be turned over to a third party for analysis, there may be a requirement for a formal request, or legal process directly requesting information in the financial institution's possession.

Once you receive the confirmation of the document being fraudulent, what are the next steps?

Discover the scope of the crime. Once the items have been deemed to be fraudulent, search every piece of information through the internal database to determine if the crime that has been committed is through a continuous course of conduct, is a wider pattern, or is a singular incident.

Are there any patterns that have been developed through analysis?

If there is a continuous course of conduct, there should be a pattern that has developed. The pattern that has been developed should help mitigate future losses, identify past conduct, but it will not eliminate future conduct. Losses will still occur, just not as great of amount.

Will this be pursued criminally, civilly, formally, or informally?

While these are not mutually exclusive and can be changed while an investigation is occurring, it is important to determine how this activity will be pursued because it determines the entities you may need to contact, both internally and externally. The type of fraud, the aggregated amount, and the means the fraudster utilized to facilitate fraud in all matters. Understanding the wishes of an employer, internal stakeholders, and external entities will assist in efficiently investigating and determining what information is needed to pursue penalties.

Practical Example Two

JJ Incorporated is a company that is in Louisiana, yet has subsidiaries in Lubbock, Texas. ABC Incorporated is a company that JJ Incorporated provided a service by repairing an item for ABC Incorporated. The cost of the service was $50,000. JJ Incorporated provided the service and then invoiced ABC Incorporated. After three months, an employee in the billing department notices that ABC Incorporated has not paid the invoice. JJ Incorporated contacts ABC Incorporated demanding payment. ABC Incorporated finds the service that was agreed upon with JJ incorporated via contract, the date JJ Incorporated performed the service, and the original invoice from services performed by JJ Incorporated. ABC Corporation also finds that after the initial invoice sent by JJ Incorporated, ABC Corporation paid JJ Incorporated 1 month after the initial invoice. This information has been sent to the auditing Department of ABC Corporation, where you are assigned the case.

What are your next actions as the assigned Auditor?

Assume that the individuals in your company, or other companies are telling the truth regarding the reported conduct, unless there are clear discrepancies. This is the only time when an assumption is made by an investigator. The investigator's role, after the reception of the complaint, is to verify the information received and that the accusations that occurred have occurred. As an auditor, you will want to ensure that the information you receive is valid.

Who are the entities involved?

Determine who the entities are in the complaint. In this case, the entities are JJ Incorporated and ABC Corporation.

What type of actions were to take place?

JJ Incorporated was to perform a service for ABC Corporation, and ABC Corporation was to pay for that service to JJ Incorporated.

Did the agreed upon action take place?

Did JJ Incorporated perform the service and did ABC Corporation pay for the service? It is important to remember that during the initial triage of an investigation and throughout certain types of investigations certain actions are contingent upon the completion of certain steps by the entities. In this case, payment for service by ABC Corporation to JJ Incorporated is contingent upon ABC Corporation as well as JJ Incorporated agreeing upon the services to be completed by JJ Incorporated, then JJ Incorporated completing those services. Once completed, ABC Corporation is to make payment.

Were there other communications or documents that preceded the actions that took place?

As an investigator, you will want to ensure that you have enough information to examine whether JJ Incorporated and ABC Corporation have an agreement. Furthermore, these documents will have individuals that have to sign or endorse these agreements.

How was payment to be made from ABC Corporation to JJ Incorporated?

ABC Incorporated was to issue payment by utilizing a financial instrument, a physical check.

Was the physical check created by ABC Corporation?

Yes or no – in this scenario, a physical check was created.

What were the identifying characteristics of the check?

The identifying characteristics of the check were the routing number of the bank institution that created the check, the payment account information, and the identifying check number which is unique. The banking institution for JJ Incorporated is Easy Bank.

Was the check sent to JJ Incorporated?

Was the check hand delivered, sent via courier or some other fashion? In this scenario, the check was sent via mail.

Was the check deposited into an account owned by JJ Incorporated?

> If JJ Incorporated is the victim and reporting entity, JJ Incorporated will, although not always, be willing to cooperate to recover their losses.

If not deposited into a JJ Incorporated account, what account was it deposited into?

> The answer to this may require legal documentation if ABC Corporation is not willing to reveal account information.

How do you get information relating to the transference of funds?

> ABC Corporation can review their own information and determine where their funds were transferred to. If the auditor is external, they may be able to ask for ABC Corporation account information regarding the specific transaction. If you are an entity external to ABC and JJ, you may be able to ask directly, but you may need to utilize other means. Administrative subpoenas, Grand Jury Subpoenas, and search warrants are tools that may be utilized.

About the Author

Jonathon Oduwole has been a peace officer in the State of Texas for several years, being employed as a Special Agent. He has investigated vehicle homicides, assaults, and numerous crimes. He has written several search warrants, arrest warrants and has consulted on numerous investigations. He has conducted simple and complex fraud investigations, as well as instructed numerous detectives, special agents, and police officers at federal and state levels.

Jonathon Oduwole has master's degrees from the University of Louisville in Justice Administration, and Amberton University in Professional Development. Jonathon Oduwole also has a bachelor's degree from the University of Louisville, Go Cardinals! He also holds numerous certifications, including being a Certified Fraud Examiner, Certified Financial Crimes Investigator, Certified Economic Crimes Forensic Examiner, and Certified Project Manager.

In his experience, he has found that public and private entities have great difficulty in grasping basic tenets of fraud investigation. Oduwole believes that while investigations can be complex, basic tenets may be able to assist in grasping fraud investigation.

Contact Jonathon Oduwole
jclogroupllc@outlook.com

www.ingramcontent.com/pod-product-compliance
Lightning Source LLC
Chambersburg PA
CBHW070813280326
41934CB00012B/3178